Land of Liberty

Utah

by Kathleen W. Deady

Consultant:
Craig Fuller
Associate Editor
Utah Historical Quarterly
Utah State Historical Society
Salt Lake City, Utah

Capstone
press
Mankato, Minnesota

Capstone Press
151 Good Counsel Drive • P.O. Box 669 • Mankato, Minnesota 56002
http://www.capstone-press.com

Library of Congress Cataloging-in-Publication Data
Deady, Kathleen W.
    Utah / by Kathleen W. Deady.
    v. cm.—(Land of Liberty)
    Includes bibliographical references and index.
    Contents: About Utah—Land, climate, and wildlife—History of Utah—
Government and politics—Economy and resources—People and culture.
    ISBN 0-7368-2200-3
    1. Utah—Juvenile literature. [1. Utah.] I. Title. II. Series.
F826.3.D43 2004
979.2—dc21   2002155826

Summary: An introduction to the geography, history, government, politics, economy,
resources, people, and culture of Utah, including maps, charts, and a recipe.

Editorial Credits
Donald Lemke, editor; Jennifer Schonborn, designer; Enoch Peterson, illustrator;
    Kelly Garvin, photo researcher; Eric Kudalis, product planning editor

Photo Credits
Cover images: Virgin River, PhotoDisc Inc.; Salt Lake City, PhotoDisc Inc.

Bruce Coleman Inc./Allan Blank, 17; Bruce Coleman Inc./Brian Miller, 8; Bruce
Coleman Inc./Joe McDonald, 57; Bruce Coleman Inc./John Elk III, 4; Capstone
Press/Gary Sundermeyer, 54; Corbis/Joseph Sohm/ChromoSohm Inc., 30–31;
Corbis/Phil Schermeister, 50–51; Folio Inc./John Coletti, 42–43; Folio Inc./Mark
Newman, 45; Getty Images Sport Services/Adam Pretty, 52; Getty Images/Hulton
Archive, 18; Hill Air Force Base, Ogden Air Logistics Center, 40; Houserstock/Dave
G. Houser, 32; Houserstock/Rankin Harvey, 38; Image Ideas Inc., 1; Index Stock
Imagery/John Coletti, 46; North Wind Picture Archives, 21, 22, 37, 58; One Mile Up
Inc., 55 (both); PhotoDisc Inc., 56, 63; Stock Montage Inc., 27; Tom Till, 12–13, 15;
Used by permission, Utah State Historical Society, all rights reserved, 25, 29; U.S.
Postal Service, 59

Artistic Effects
Corbis, Image Ideas, PhotoDisc Inc.

1 2 3 4 5 6 08 07 06 05 04 03

Table of Contents

The Salt Lake Temple serves as a place of worship for members of The Church of Jesus Christ of Latter-day Saints.

Chapter 1

About Utah

In 1847, a group of religious people designed a grand city in the middle of a desert. The Mormons had moved to Utah for religious freedom. At the center of the city, they built the 10-acre (4-hectare) Temple Square.

Today, Temple Square is one of the most visited attractions in Utah. Mormons visit Temple Square to worship and hold religious ceremonies. Others visit the area to view the famous Salt Lake Temple.

Completed in 1893, the Salt Lake Temple took more than 40 years to build. The temple has six tall spires. The tallest spire reaches 210 feet (64 meters) into the air. Only faithful

Mormons are allowed to enter the historic temple.

The Beehive State

The construction of the Salt Lake Temple shows the Mormons' belief in hard work and community. The honeybee was a symbol of these beliefs. When the Mormons first came to the area, they named their settlement Deseret, meaning honeybee. Although the name was later changed to Utah, the state's nickname is the Beehive State.

Utah's position between Nevada and Colorado puts it in the heart of the West. As the 13th largest state, Utah stretches from Idaho and Wyoming in the north to Arizona and New Mexico in the south.

The corners of New Mexico, Utah, Colorado, and Arizona all come together at a single point. This point is the only place in the country where four states meet. One person can stand in all four states at the same time. The Four Corners Monument marks this spot.

Utah Cities

IDAHO

NEVADA

WYOMING

COLORADO

ARIZONA

NEW MEXICO

UTAH

● Logan

Brigham City ●

Ogden ●

Salt Lake City ✪

● Tooele

● Provo

Roosevelt ●

● Nephi

● Richfield

● Moab

● Cedar City

● St. George

Four Corners Monument

Scale
Miles

0	30	60	90

Kilometers

0	30	60	90	120

N
W E
S

Legend

▇	American Indian Reservation
✪	Capital
●	City
○	Point of Interest

In late September, leaves in the Uinta National Forest turn a variety of colors.

Chapter 2

Land, Climate, and Wildlife

Utah is part of three very different land areas. They are the Rocky Mountains, the Basin and Range Region, and the Colorado Plateau. These regions offer snowcapped mountains and large deserts. They also have wide-open prairies and deep, rocky canyons.

The U.S. government owns almost 63 percent of Utah. Five national parks and six national forests lie entirely within the state's borders. Utah also shares three national forests with neighboring states.

The Rocky Mountains

Two ranges of the Rocky Mountains run through northeastern Utah. The Uinta Mountains stretch from Colorado westward toward Salt Lake City. Several peaks in this range are more than 13,000 feet (3,960 meters) high. Kings Peak, at 13,534 feet (4,125 meters), is the highest point in Utah.

The Wasatch Range of the Rocky Mountains extends south from Idaho. It meets the Uinta Range near Nephi. The eastern side of the Wasatch Range rises gently to the mountain peaks. The western side of the range has steep walls and cliffs. The cliffs drop sharply 6,000 to 8,000 feet (1,825 to 2,440 meters) to the flatlands of the Basin and Range Region.

The Basin and Range Region

The Basin and Range Region extends westward from the Wasatch Range. This area is one of the driest areas in the country. It is mostly desert. The Great Salt Lake Desert, the Sevier Desert, and the Escalante Desert are all part of the Basin and Range Region. These areas are mostly dry, treeless valleys called basins. Beaverdam Creek, in southwestern Utah, is the lowest point in the state. It is 2,350 feet (716 meters) above sea level.

Utah's Land Features

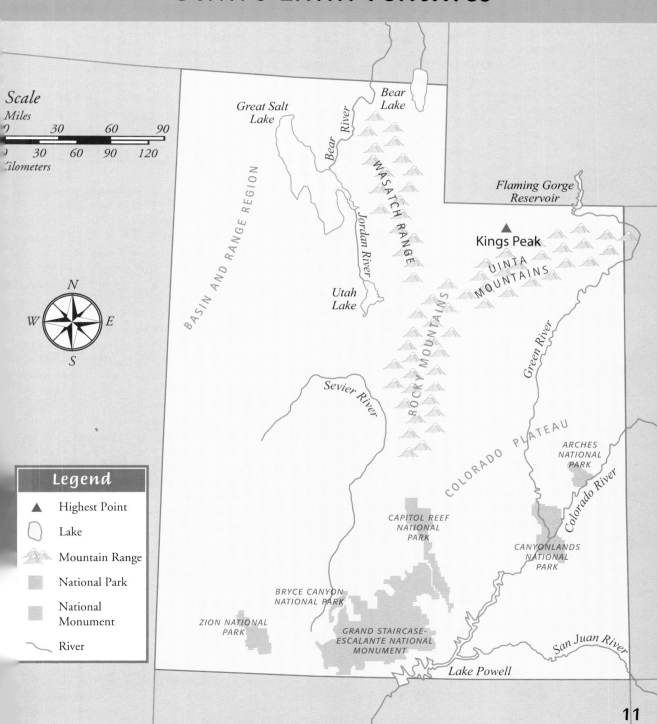

Scale

Miles
0   30   60   90

Kilometers
0   30   60   90   120

Legend

▲ Highest Point

Lake

Mountain Range

National Park

National Monument

River

Great Salt Lake

Bear River

Bear Lake

Flaming Gorge Reservoir

Jordan River

WASATCH RANGE

Kings Peak ▲

UINTA MOUNTAINS

Utah Lake

BASIN AND RANGE REGION

ROCKY MOUNTAINS

Green River

Sevier River

COLORADO PLATEAU

ARCHES NATIONAL PARK

Colorado River

CAPITOL REEF NATIONAL PARK

CANYONLANDS NATIONAL PARK

BRYCE CANYON NATIONAL PARK

ZION NATIONAL PARK

GRAND STAIRCASE-ESCALANTE NATIONAL MONUMENT

San Juan River

Lake Powell

N
W   E
S

The Colorado Plateau

The Colorado Plateau stretches over eastern and southern Utah into northern Arizona, western Colorado, and northwestern New Mexico. The Colorado Plateau is a broad, rocky highland. Some of the highest plateaus in Utah are more than 11,000 feet (3,350 meters) above sea level. Deep, jagged canyons and valleys cut through the plateaus. Large cliffs show layers of different colored rocks. Wind and water have carved arches, bridges, and towering rock formations in this region.

In the winter, visitors to Dead Horse Point State Park can see snow in the deep canyons. The park is located 2,000 feet (610 meters) above the Colorado River.

Rivers and Lakes

Many of the rivers and lakes in Utah provide water for farmland. Some of this farmland would otherwise be dry and useless. The Colorado River and the Green River are Utah's largest rivers. Except for the Bear River, all of the water from eastern Utah drains into these two rivers. Water from the Bear River flows into the Great Salt Lake.

Utah has had several lakes that are salty from minerals in the soil. The largest is the Great Salt Lake. The other saltwater lakes dried up when farmers redirected water for irrigation.

Did you know...?
The salt industries in Utah take out about 2.5 million tons (2.3 million metric tons) of sodium chloride and other minerals from the Great Salt Lake every year.

The largest natural freshwater lakes in the state are Utah Lake and Bear Lake. Water flows out of Bear Lake into the Bear River. The Jordan River drains Utah Lake into the Great Salt Lake. Bear Lake and Utah Lake are important water supplies for the state. Many smaller lakes are also spread throughout the Uinta and Wasatch Mountains and the high plateaus of Utah.

Climate

Utah is the second driest state, after Nevada. The amount of rain, snow, and other moisture varies greatly across the state. The Great Salt Lake Desert averages less than 6 inches (15 centimeters) of precipitation each year. The Wasatch Mountains near Salt Lake City can receive more than 50 inches (127 centimeters) of rain each year. During the winter, as much as 400 inches (1,016 centimeters) of snow can fall in this part of the state.

Temperatures in Utah are warm in the summer and cool in the winter. The average summer temperature is 69 degrees

The Great Salt Lake

The Great Salt Lake is 3 to 5 times saltier than the ocean. Minerals in the soil around the lake make it salty. The salt in the water allows swimmers to float for long periods of time. It is even difficult to swim under the water.

The Great Salt Lake is the largest saltwater lake in North America. It is also one of the largest in the world. The lake is about 75 miles (121 kilometers) long and 35 miles (56 kilometers) wide. It covers 1,700 square miles (4,403 square kilometers).

Fahrenheit (21 degrees Celsius). The average temperature in winter is 27 degrees Fahrenheit (minus 3 degrees Celsius).

Utah often gets thunderstorms on summer afternoons. Many of these storms do not have rain. The rain often turns into a gas, or evaporates, in the hot air before it reaches the ground. This unusual event is called virga. Virgas are common over the plateaus.

Plants and Animals

Forests cover about 29 percent of Utah. Forests grow mainly in the mountainous areas of the state. The mountains support a wide variety of trees. These trees include aspens, pines, poplars, spruce, and junipers. The hardy piñon pine can survive at 7,500 feet (2,286 meters) above sea level. Great Basin bristlecone pines can grow on mountain ledges at 10,000 to 11,000 feet (3,050 to 3,350 meters). Some of these short and twisted trees are more than 3,000 years old.

Cactuses, low shrubs, grasses, and wildflowers grow in the drier areas of the state. A common tangled shrub called sagebrush grows 3 to 6 feet (1 to 2 meters) high. Wildflowers include yuccas and desert sunrays. The state flower, the sego lily, also grows in these areas. It can have white, purple, or yellow blossoms.

Utah is home to a wide variety of large animals. Black bears, elk, moose, and pronghorn antelopes roam the forests and canyons. Small herds of buffalo live in national parks, Antelope Island State Park, and on a few private ranches. Wild horses called mustangs live in the desert valleys. Coyotes and mountain lions thrive in the mountains.

The Gila monster is the largest lizard native to the United States. Adult Gila monsters average more than 20 inches (51 centimeters) in length. They live in the deserts of southern Utah.

Many types of birds are found throughout the state. The roadrunner is an unusual bird found in southwestern Utah. Since it is a weak flyer, the roadrunner scurries along the ground hunting for rattlesnakes and other prey.

Besides rattlesnakes, the desert supports many other reptiles. These reptiles include tortoises and lizards called Gila monsters.

In 1860, a Shoshone family was photographed near Salt Lake City. Many American Indians lived in the Utah area before the arrival of Spanish explorers.

Chapter 3

History of Utah

By the 1700s, four major American Indian groups lived in the area that is now Utah. The Ute lived in the eastern part of the area. The Paiute lived in the west. The Shoshone lived in the northwest. A subgroup of the Shoshone, called the Goshute, lived in the west-central part of the area. These groups each had many smaller divisions with separate chiefs.

Early Explorers

The first explorers to come to the Utah area were Spanish. In 1765, Juan Maria de Rivera explored southeastern Utah. Spain controlled much of the land in this region. Spanish lands stretched from Central America north to the area of

Santa Fe, New Mexico. The Spanish had also settled in the area of California. These California settlements could only be reached by sea.

In 1776, Silvestre Velez de Escalante and Francisco Atanasio Dominguez left Santa Fe. These Spanish priests explored Utah, looking for an easy land route to California. They struggled for months to find a route. Instead, they found mountain peaks and steep-walled canyons. In 1777, they gave up and returned to Santa Fe.

In 1821, Mexico won independence from Spain. Mexico took control of the areas of Utah, Nevada, California, Arizona, New Mexico, southern Colorado, and Texas.

At the same time, European hunters and traders came to the Utah area for beaver fur. Beaver fur was in great demand by hat and coat makers. In 1824, Jim Bridger was probably the first white man to see the Great Salt Lake. By about 1840, Bridger and other Europeans had left the area. Many of these men went searching for better land.

Locating the First Settlement

The first people to settle in Utah were the Mormons. The Mormons are members of The Church of Jesus Christ of

Latter-day Saints. In 1830, Joseph Smith Jr. founded the church in New York.

The Mormons had many strong beliefs. One belief was that Mormon men could have more than one wife at a time. This practice is called polygamy. Many people disagreed with Mormon beliefs. Wherever the Mormons went, people harassed them because of their beliefs.

The Mormons moved to Ohio and Missouri and eventually settled in Illinois. In 1844, an angry mob destroyed the Mormons' farms and killed Joseph Smith Jr.

In 1830, Joseph Smith Jr. established The Church of Jesus Christ of Latter-day Saints.

In 1847, Brigham Young, with arm raised, and other Mormons arrived in the Salt Lake Valley. They had traveled more than 1,000 miles (1,610 kilometers) across the Great Plains.

In 1846, the new Mormon leader, Brigham Young, led the Mormons west in search of a new home.

In July 1847, the Mormons reached the Great Salt Lake Valley. Even though the land was harsh and dry, the Mormons believed they could build a glorious city in the area. They also thought they had left the United States. With no Mexican settlements in the area, they ignored Mexico's claims to the land. They wanted this new homeland to be an independent Mormon nation.

As the Mormons settled in the Salt Lake Valley, the United States fought the Mexican War (1846–1848) with Mexico. On February 2, 1848, the war ended with the Treaty of Guadalupe Hidalgo. This treaty gave large amounts of land to the United States, including the area of Utah. The Mormons were once again on land controlled by the United States.

Becoming a Territory

The Mormons worked very hard to settle their new home. They built irrigation ditches, which carried water from rivers to dry land. They plowed the land and planted crops. They built shelters of sun-dried adobe bricks. The Mormons also began building the city of their dreams. They called it Great Salt Lake City, after the nearby lake.

In 1849, the Mormons named their new land the State of Deseret. The State of Deseret included parts of nine future states. The Mormons set up a government with Brigham Young as governor.

By 1850, the Mormon population had grown to 11,000. Besides Salt Lake City, the Mormons settled Ogden, Provo, Manti, and Tooele. They started the University of Deseret, later called the University of Utah. They also started Utah's first newspaper, *The Deseret News.*

The Mormons knew they could not stay completely independent. But they still hoped for a Mormon state. They asked Congress to admit the State of Deseret to the Union. In 1850, Congress turned down both the request and the name Deseret. Instead, Congress created a smaller territory named the Utah Territory. Utah's boundaries changed several times. In 1868, Congress established Utah's boundaries as they are today.

Indian Conflicts

As the population of the Utah Territory grew, problems started with American Indian tribes. The Indians in Utah felt the settlers were taking their land. In July 1853, Ute Indians began attacking the settlers. These attacks became known as the Walker War (1853–1854). The Walker War was named for the Ute chief, Walkara. Finally in 1854, Brigham Young and Walkara met and made peace.

The Indians and Mormons fought again in the Tintic Indian War (1856) and in the Black Hawk War (1865–1868). The Indians were eventually defeated. The U.S. government removed the American Indians to the Uintah and Ouray Reservation in eastern Utah.

Beginning in 1865, Chief Black Hawk and other Utes fought against Mormon pioneers in the Black Hawk War. In 1867, Chief Black Hawk met with the Mormons and made peace. The war officially ended in 1868.

Conflict with the Government

Conflicts and mistrust also grew between the Mormons and the U.S. government. Many people were shocked by Mormon customs, including polygamy. U.S. President James Buchanan believed Mormons were rebelling and breaking U.S. laws. He wanted to take control of Utah from the Mormons. In 1857, Buchanan appointed Alfred Cumming of Georgia as the new governor of Utah Territory. He sent Cumming with troops to Utah to enforce U.S. laws. This action started what was called the Utah War (1857–1858).

The Mormons believed their church laws were above the laws made by men. They prepared to defend themselves. The Mormons sent scouts ahead to find the U.S. soldiers. They burned army supply wagons and delayed the soldiers' arrival.

Eventually, the U.S. troops were able to build a camp near Salt Lake City. In 1857, Brigham Young agreed to step down as governor. The army stayed in Utah until the Civil War (1861–1865) began in the east.

Change and Growth

After the Utah War, the territory became more connected with the rest of the country. By 1869, railroad lines came

On May 10, 1869, the Union Pacific and the Central Pacific Railroads met at Promontory Summit. The event marked the completion of the first transcontinental railroad.

to the territory from the east and from the west. The transcontinental railroad connected at Promontory Summit in Utah Territory. The increased transportation brought new trade opportunities and more settlers to the area.

In the late 1860s, gold and silver were discovered in the mountains of Utah. This discovery brought a flood of miners and prospectors to the area. By 1880, the Utah Territory population was more than 143,000.

From Territory to State

During the late 1800s, Utah tried several times for statehood. Congress continued to say no because the Mormons practiced polygamy. In 1880, Congress outlawed polygamy. The Mormons refused to follow the new law. The government jailed more than 1,000 polygamists and would not let many Mormons vote. In 1890, the Mormon Church finally outlawed polygamy.

In 1895, Utahns held a convention in Salt Lake City. They wrote a state constitution. Besides outlawing polygamy, the constitution also gave women the right to vote. By 1896, only Utah, Wyoming, Colorado, and Idaho had given women this right. Utah became the 45th state on January 4, 1896.

Early Twentieth Century

By 1900, Utah's population was more than 276,000 and growing. Many ethnic groups came to the state. They included Greeks, Japanese, Hispanics, and African Americans.

In 1917, the United States entered World War I (1914–1918). Around 20,000 Utahns served in the war. At home, workers used metal from Utah's mines to make weapons. An economic boom continued for a period after the war. Utah developed a new tourist industry. Better roads brought many people to see Utah's natural features. By 1930, Utah's population had grown to more than 500,000.

The Great Depression (1929–1939) hit the economy of both Utah and the country very hard. Mines, banks, and businesses closed. Many people lost their jobs.

Between 1900 and 1930, the population of Salt Lake City almost tripled. Electric trolleys helped people travel around the growing city.

Better Times

World War II (1939–1945) helped Utah recover from the Great Depression. Crop prices rose. Mines and factories reopened to make tanks, weapons, uniforms, and other products for war. Many people came to work at military bases in Utah. These bases included Hill Air Force Base in northern Utah and Fort Douglas in Salt Lake City.

After the war, the mining industry grew when workers found uranium near Moab in 1952. Uranium is used in nuclear power plants and nuclear weapons.

Utah Today

Slowly, the economy continued to improve with the growth of high-tech jobs. In 1983, several people from Utah started the Novell company. They developed a program that let computers communicate with each other. Soon, other high-tech companies made Utah an important center for the computer industry. These companies included WordPerfect, Iomega, and Unisys.

Today, Utah has one of the fastest growing economies and lowest jobless rates in the country. It also has one of the fastest growing populations.

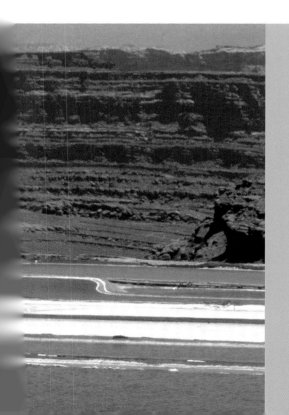

A uranium mine pond near Moab holds water used during mining.

Completed in 1916, the Utah State Capitol overlooks downtown Salt Lake City.

Chapter 4

Government and Politics

The Mormons had a vision for Utah. They wanted a government and economy shaped and run by the church. When the state adopted its constitution in 1895, the Mormons made many compromises. The constitution included a law banning polygamy. It also separated the church from government, as does the U.S. Constitution. Today, Utah's government is separate from the church.

State Government

Utah's state government is set up like the U.S. government. It is divided into three branches. They are the executive, the legislative, and the judicial branches.

The executive branch is led by the governor. Since 1994, the governor is limited to three terms. Each term is four years long. After 12 consecutive years in office, the governor cannot seek reelection.

The legislative branch includes both the senate and the house of representatives. The senate has 29 members. The house of representatives has 75 members. These people help make the laws for the state of Utah.

The judicial branch is divided into many different courts. The supreme court, the highest court in Utah, is made up of five justices. Lower courts include the court of appeals, the district court, the juvenile court, and justice courts.

Politics Today

Utah has been a leader in political opportunity for women. In 1895, Utah gave women the right to vote. In 1896, Martha Hughes Cannon became the first woman state senator in the country. As a doctor, Cannon worked in the senate to create a State Board of Health.

Utah's State Government

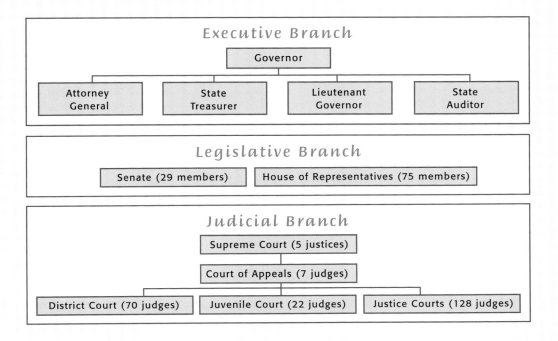

Executive Branch

- Governor
  - Attorney General
  - State Treasurer
  - Lieutenant Governor
  - State Auditor

Legislative Branch

- Senate (29 members)
- House of Representatives (75 members)

Judicial Branch

- Supreme Court (5 justices)
- Court of Appeals (7 judges)
  - District Court (70 judges)
  - Juvenile Court (22 judges)
  - Justice Courts (128 judges)

Utah has had some well-known elected officials. Edwin Jacob Garn served in the U.S. Senate from 1974 to 1993. He was also an astronaut. In 1985, he traveled in space and orbited Earth 109 times in the space shuttle Discovery. Republican Orrin Hatch was elected to the U.S. Senate in 1976. Hatch supports both religious freedom and health care reform.

Brigham Young

Brigham Young (1801–1877) was a religious and political leader for the early settlers of Utah. Young was a carpenter and a painter when he was first drawn into the Mormon religion. In 1832, he was baptized into The Church of Jesus Christ of Latter-day Saints. He quickly gained respect as a preacher in the church.

In 1844, Young took over as the church leader when its founder, Joseph Smith Jr., was murdered. Young was determined to find a home for his people. He wanted it to be a place where Mormons could live and worship freely.

Young was more than an inspiring religious leader. He took charge of organizing thousands of Mormons on their journey. He led the first group across the Great Plains and the Rocky Mountains to Salt Lake City. He later returned and brought more Mormons who were waiting to join the others.

Young organized the political, economic, and cultural affairs of the Mormons in their new home. He led them in developing irrigation systems and building their farms. He helped them start small businesses and stores. He set up schools and organized the first government for the settlements.

Brigham Young became the leader of The Church of Jesus Christ of Latter-day Saints in 1844. During his life, Young led the immigration of more than 70,000 people to Utah.

Young served as governor of the Utah Territory from 1850 to 1857. He remained in control of the church until he died in 1877.

Skiing is a popular activity for Utah residents and visitors. A large part of the state's money comes from service industries, such as tourism.

Chapter 5

Economy and Resources

Until the 1900s, agriculture was the most important part of Utah's economy. The state has changed a great deal since its early days. In recent years, Utah has become less dependent on farming. The economy has grown in service industries, manufacturing, and mining. Today, Utah has one of the fastest-growing economies in the country.

Service Industries

Service industries contribute the most money to Utah's economy. Service industry workers help people and serve the public. Business, community, and personal services make up

Hill Air Force Base, Ogden Air Logistics Center is located in northern Utah. Some workers at Hill Air Force Base repair and maintain Air Force equipment.

the largest part of the service industry. These businesses include private health care, law firms, repair shops, and tourist sites.

Tourism became a successful industry during the 1960s and 1970s. Many national parks and ski resorts opened

throughout the state. In 2002, Utah had five national parks and fourteen ski resorts. These resorts offer some of the best skiing in the world. They attract thousands of visitors every year.

Banks and real estate companies make up the second largest part of the service industry. Salt Lake City is the financial center of Utah. Wells Fargo, the state's largest bank, is located in Salt Lake City. Many Utahns also work at several major credit card companies. Utah's population growth has caused a need for many new homes. This has brought a big boost to real estate businesses.

Government services are another section of the service industry. Government workers include teachers, hospital workers, postal workers, and military personnel. Hill Air Force Base is one of Utah's leading employers. Many people also work for the government in state parks and forests.

Agriculture and Mining

Today, agriculture is a much smaller part of Utah's economy. Less than 2 percent of Utahns work in agriculture. But the state still has more than 13,000 farms. These farms cover about 20 percent of Utah's total land area. Most of the farmland is in the fertile areas west of the Wasatch Range. More than 1,000,000 acres (405,000 hectares) of farmland are irrigated. Farmers grow grasses and grains to feed livestock. They also grow potatoes, onions, other vegetables, and fruits.

Livestock and their products provide about three-quarters of Utah's agricultural income. Beef cattle and milk are the leading products. Utah is also one of the top sheep-farming states. Huge grazing areas are used for raising sheep and cattle.

Mining is also an important part of Utah's economy. The state is rich in natural resources. Coal, natural gas, uranium, petroleum, and natural salts are all found in Utah. Petroleum and natural gas are mostly found in the northeastern part of the state.

Salt is piled on the ground near Grantsville, Utah. Many types of salt are found throughout the state. These salts are used for softening water, de-icing roads, and seasoning food.

Many valuable metals are also mined in the state. Utah is the second-leading copper producing state in the country. Most of the copper is mined at the Bingham Canyon west of Salt Lake City. At 2.5 miles (4 kilometers) wide, it is one of the largest open-pit copper mines in the world. Gold and silver are also mined in Utah.

Manufacturing

Manufacturing is the second largest part of Utah's economy. Most manufacturing plants are located between Brigham City and Provo. Many of these plants are near Salt Lake City.

Manufacturing companies in Utah make many different products. These products include computer and office equipment. Transportation equipment is also a leading manufactured product. Many companies developed with the military defense industry in the late 1950s. Military products include solid fuel for missiles, rockets, and jet engines. Other products include medical equipment and navigational systems for airplanes and ships.

The Land Debate

In recent years, many people have debated how Utah's land should be used. Some feel mining for natural resources will create jobs for Utahns. Others favor using the land for recreational activities, such as ski resorts. Environmentalists want to leave the land untouched.

In 1996, President Clinton declared 1,900,000 acres (770,000 hectares) in southern Utah a national monument. Some people supported the creation of the Grand Staircase-Escalante National Monument. Others were strongly opposed. As Utah's population increases, such debates are likely to continue.

Food processing is another major area of manufacturing. Some companies make processed food products such as cheese and baked goods. Other companies include flour mills and meatpacking plants.

Salt Lake City is the center for business in the state. It is also the largest city in Utah, with more than 200,000 people.

Chapter 6

People and Culture

Utah has one of the fastest growing populations in the country. The state also has one of the highest percentages of city residents in the country. Most of the population lives in cities along the Wasatch Front. The Wasatch Front is the area west of the Wasatch Range in north-central Utah. The rest of the population is scattered in rural parts of the state. Although the population of Utah is largely urban, the state's cities are fairly small. Only Salt Lake City, West Valley City, and Provo have more than 100,000 people each.

"And though it was once a desert in the middle of nowhere, it is now a city in the middle of nowhere, and Salt Lake City likes its splendid isolation from other places. . ."
—*Stephen Birmingham, 1978,* The Golden Dream

Ethnic and Religious Diversity

Most of Utah's first settlers were of the same ethnic background. Almost all were white and came from northern European ancestors. Although most of Utah's population is still white, people of other ethnic backgrounds have moved to the state.

Today, about 93 percent of Utahns were born in America. According to the 2000 U.S. census, almost 9 out of every 10 Utahns are white. These Utahns are mostly of English, German, and Scandinavian backgrounds. Hispanics are the second largest group and the fastest growing minority. They make up about 9 percent of the population. A small group of Utahns, about 1.6 percent, is Asian. Less than 1 percent of Utahns are African American.

A little more than 1 percent of Utahns are American Indian. They are mostly Navajo, Ute, Goshute, or Shoshone. Many American Indians in Utah live on the Uintah and Ouray Reservation in the east. They also live on the Navajo

Utah's Ethnic Backgrounds

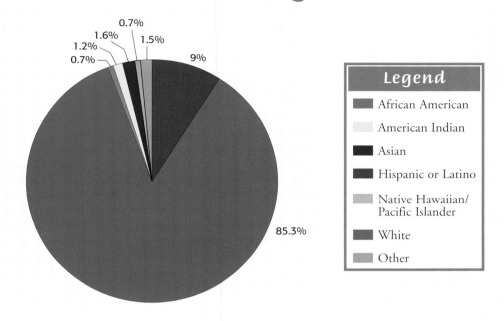

0.7%
1.6%
1.2%
0.7%
1.5%
9%
85.3%

Legend

- African American
- American Indian
- Asian
- Hispanic or Latino
- Native Hawaiian/ Pacific Islander
- White
- Other

Reservation in the south. Some American Indians live on smaller reservations in the western part of the state.

Utah is still about 70 percent Mormon, but people of many other religions also live there. Roman Catholics make up the second largest religious group. Many Protestant groups also live in Utah. They include Baptists, Presbyterians, Methodists, and Episcopalians. A smaller number of Utahns are Jewish.

Music, Arts, and Sports

Utahns make many contributions to the arts. One of the most famous cultural organizations is the Mormon Tabernacle Choir. This choir has made many recordings of its music. It has broadcast concerts on the radio since 1929. Utah also has several well-known music and dance companies. They include the Utah Symphony, Ballet West, and the Utah Opera.

Utahns love sports, especially basketball. They are very proud of their major professional sports team, the Utah Jazz. This basketball team moved to Utah from New Orleans

Formed in 1869, the Mormon Tabernacle Choir has more than 300 members. The choir has performed at five presidential inaugurations and produced more than 150 recordings.

in 1979. It has produced several stars, including forward Karl Malone and point guard John Stockton. Utah also hosted the 2002 Olympic Winter Games.

The Mormon Way of Life

The Mormon population has a big influence on the state. Since territorial times, Mormons have been a majority of the state's population. One reason is that Mormons believe in large families. Utah has the highest birthrate in the country.

Olympics in Salt Lake

SALT LAKE 2002

Salt Lake City hosted the 2002 Olympic Winter Games. The state built new highways to handle the large amount of traffic. Utahns also built the Olympic Village on the campus of the University of Utah.

Salt Lake City was the center of the Olympic activities. Many other towns hosted events as well. Speed skating took place in Kearns. Park City hosted the giant slalom and snow boarding. Women's hockey was held in Provo, and curling took place in Ogden.

Another reason is that many Mormons move to Utah. Most people that come to the state are Mormons.

Mormon churches do not have pastors or priests as leaders. Instead, church members lead activities. Mormons also run active missionary programs around the world. At age 19, young men spend two years away from home. Some young women, at the age of 21, spend eighteen months away from home. They travel around the world and teach others about their faith. They work hard to bring new people into the church.

The Mormon Church teaches its people a positive lifestyle. It teaches them not to drink alcohol or smoke. It also teaches them to work hard and live a simple lifestyle. Mormons believe strongly in a commitment to marriage. They also stress the importance of family life and helping other people.

Mormons believe education is very important. As a result, Utah has one of the highest literacy rates in the country. It has one of the highest percentages of high school graduates. Utah also has a higher than average percentage of college students.

For more than 100 years, the natural beauty of Utah has drawn people from around the world. The first settlers in Utah were hardworking and determined. They saw a land that was harsh and dry, a land that no one else wanted. By working together, they built Utah into a thriving state. Today, the state's healthy economy and family lifestyle attract people from a variety of cultures.

Recipe: Green Jell-O Salad

In 2001, the Utah legislature named Jell-O the official state snack. Jell-O salads are popular desserts at family gatherings and Mormon church events. The state snack is often served with fruits or vegetables.

Ingredients

2 cups (480 mL) boiling water
1 6-ounce (165-gram) package lime gelatin dessert
½ teaspoon (2.5 mL) salt
1½ cups (360 mL) cold water
1 tablespoon (15 mL) vinegar
2 cups (480 mL) shredded carrots

Equipment

medium saucepan
liquid measuring cup
large mixing bowl
large spoon
decorative bowl or mold
dry-ingredient measuring cup

What You Do

1. In medium saucepan, heat 2 cups of water on high heat until boiling.

2. In large mixing bowl, combine gelatin and salt.

3. With a large spoon, stir boiling water into gelatin mixture for at least 2 minutes or until gelatin is completely dissolved.

4. Add cold water and vinegar; stir.

5. Pour mixture into a decorative bowl or mold, if desired.

6. Refrigerate gelatin mixture for 1½ hours or until gelatin is slightly thickened.

7. With a large spoon, stir in shredded carrots.

8. Refrigerate for an additional 4 hours or until firm.

Makes 8 ½-cup servings

Utah's Flag and Seal

Utah's Flag

The original state flag was adopted in 1896. It was later revised and made official in 1913. The flag is dark blue with a yellow circle in the middle. Inside the circle is the state seal.

Utah's State Seal

The Utah legislature approved the state seal in 1896. On a shield in the middle is a beehive, which stands for hard work. Sego lilies, representing peace, surround the hive. Below the hive is the year 1847. This was the year Mormons first came to Utah. Above the beehive is the word "Industry," the state motto. Above the motto are six arrows and a bald eagle, representing protection. Two U.S. flags surround the shield. Around the border are the words "The Great Seal of the State of Utah." The date 1896, at the bottom, is when Utah became a state.

Almanac

General Facts

Nickname: Beehive State

Population: 2,233,169 (U.S. Census 2000)
Population rank: 34th

Capital: Salt Lake City

Largest cities: Salt Lake City, West Valley City, Provo, Sandy, Orem

Geography

Area: 84,904 square miles (219,901 square kilometers)
Size rank: 13th

Highest point: Kings Peak, 13,534 feet (4,125 meters) above sea level

Lowest point: Beaverdam Creek in Washington County, 2,350 feet (716 meters) above sea level

Agriculture

Agricultural products: Milk, beef, turkeys, eggs, hogs, sheep, cattle feed, wheat, barley, corn, apples, peaches, potatoes, nursery products

Climate

Average winter temperature: 27 degrees Fahrenheit (minus 3 degrees Celsius)

Average summer temperature: 69 degrees Fahrenheit (21 degrees Celsius)

Average annual precipitation: 11 inches (28 centimeters)

Cherries

California seagulls

Economy

Natural resources:
Coal, natural gas, petroleum, uranium, copper, gold, silver, limestone

Types of industry:
Service, manufacturing, agriculture, mining

Government

First governor: Heber Manning Wells, 1896–1905

Statehood:
January 4, 1896 (45th state)

U.S. Representatives: 3

U.S. Senators: 2

U.S. electoral votes: 5

Counties: 29

Symbols

Animal: Rocky Mountain elk

Bird: California seagull

Emblem: Beehive

Flower: Sego lily

Fruit: Cherry

Gem: Topaz

Symbols

Insect: Honeybee

Mineral: Copper

Rock: Coal

Song: "Utah This is the Place," by Sam and Gary Francis

Tree: Blue spruce

Vegetable: Spanish sweet onion

Timeline

State History

1776
Silvestre Velez de Escalante and Francisco Atanasio Dominguez reach Utah while looking for a land route from the area of Santa Fe, New Mexico to California.

1765
Spaniard Juan Maria de Rivera explores southeastern Utah.

1857–1858
Mormons and the U.S. government fight in the Utah War.

1847
Mormons reach the Great Salt Lake Valley.

1896
Utah becomes the 45th state on January 4th.

U.S. History

1775–1783
American colonies fight for independence from Great Britain in the Revolutionary War.

1846–1848
The United States fights Mexico in the Mexican War.

1861–1865
Union states fight Confederate states in the Civil War.

1620
The Pilgrims establish a colony in North America.

1812–1814
The United States fights Great Britain in the War of 1812.

1916

Workers complete the Utah State Capitol in Salt Lake City.

1983

A group of Utahns start the Novell company with an idea for a new computer program.

1996

President Bill Clinton creates the Grand Staircase-Escalante National Monument.

1952

Workers find uranium deposits near Moab.

2002

Salt Lake City hosts the 2002 Olympic Winter Games.

1929–1939

The United States experiences the Great Depression.

1964

U.S. Congress passes the Civil Rights Act, which makes discrimination illegal.

1914–1918

World War I is fought; the United States enters the war in 1917.

1939–1945

World War II is fought; the United States enters the war in 1941.

2001

On September 11, terrorists attack the World Trade Center and the Pentagon.

Words to Know

canyon (KAN-yuhn)—a deep and narrow valley with steep sides

evaporate (e-VAP-uh-rate)—the action of a liquid changing into vapor or a gas; heat causes water to evaporate.

fertile (FUR-tuhl)—good for growing crops; fertile soil has many nutrients.

irrigate (IHR-uh-gate)—to supply dry land with water through ditches, pipes, or streams

motto (MOT-oh)—a word or saying that expresses the goals and ideals of people or a nation

polygamy (puh-LIG-uh-mee)—the practice of having more than one wife or husband at the same time

range (RAYNJ)—a large group or chain of mountains

reservoir (REZ-ur-vwar)—a natural or artificial holding area for storing a large amount of water

temple (TEM-puhl)—a building used for worship

To Learn More

Gunderson, Cory Gideon. *Brigham Young: Pioneer and Prophet.* Let Freedom Ring. Mankato, Minn.: Bridgestone Books, 2003.

Haberle, Susan E. *The Mexican War, 1846–1848.* Mankato, Minn.: Bridgestone Books, 2003.

Neri, P. J. *Utah.* From Sea to Shining Sea. New York: Children's Press, 2002.

Stefoff, Rebecca. *Utah.* Celebrate the States. New York: Benchmark Books, 2001.

Internet Sites

Do you want to find out more about Utah?
Let FactHound, our fact-finding hound dog, do the research for you.

Here's how:
1) Visit *http://www.facthound.com*
2) Type in the **Book ID** number:
   0736822003
3) Click on **FETCH IT.**

FactHound will fetch Internet sites picked by our editors just for you!

Places to Write and Visit

Arches National Park
P.O. Box 907
Moab, UT 84532-0907

Escalante Chamber of Commerce
P.O. Box 175
Escalante, UT 84726

Golden Spike National Historic Site
P.O. Box 897
Brigham City, UT 84302-0897

Salt Lake Convention & Visitors Bureau
Salt Palace Convention Center
90 South West Temple
Salt Lake City, UT 84101

Utah Division of Wildlife Resources
1594 West North Temple
Salt Lake City, UT 84114

Utah State Historical Society
300 South Rio Grande Street
Salt Lake City, UT 84101

Delicate Arch is one of many natural rock formations in Arches National Park.

Index